**Pictures
to share**

**Pictures
to share**

First published in 2009 by
Pictures to Share Community Interest Company,
a UK based social enterprise that publishes
illustrated books for older people.

www.picturestoshare.co.uk

ISBN 978-0-9553940-8-9

Pets
in pictures

Edited by Helen J Bate

What's the use of worrying?

It never was worth while...

Quotation: from the lyrics to one of the songs definitively synonymous with the First World War, Pack up your Troubles. Written by George Asaf

The chickens are coming home to roost...

Photographs: Chicken walking into the house. © Peter Cade/Iconica/Getty Images

Quotation: Douglas MacArthur (1880 -1964) Comment to John F Kennedy on the presidential crisis 1965

Queen Elizabeth II
of the United Kingdom
with the
Queen Mother
and the royal Corgis

To be trusted

is a greater compliment
than to be loved.

Painting: Alice Antoinette de la Mar, aged five (oil on canvas)
by Jan van Beers (1852 - 1927). The Bridgeman Art Library/Getty Images

Quotation: George MacDonald, The Marquis of Lossie. (1824 - 1905)

ALICE·ANTOINETTE·DE·LA·MAR·ABOUT·THE·AGE·OF·5·   JAN VAN BEERS

Children

have neither past
nor future;

They enjoy the present,
which very few
of us do.

Photograph: Two young boys feed George
the giant tortoise at London Zoo 1948.
© PA Photos/PA Archive/Press Association Images

Quotation: Jean de la Bruyere (1645 - 1696)
www.quotegarden.com

Girls play with
a pet monkey
in Congo, Africa.

I had a little pony

His name was Dapple-grey
I lent him to a lady
To ride a mile away.

She whipped him, she lashed him,
She rode him through the mire.
I wouldn't lend my pony now,
For all the lady's hire.

Photograph: © Animal Photography / Sally Anne Thompson
Text. I had a Little Pony. Anonymous rhyme

Animals are such agreeable friends;
they ask no questions,
they pass no criticisms.

Photograph: Man holding cat. © Sam Bassett/Stone/Getty Images

Quotation: George Eliot, 'Mr. Gilfil's Love Story,' Scenes of Clerical Life,
1857 English novelist (1819 - 1880)

Would you like to swing on a star
Carry moonbeams home in a jar
And be better off than you are

Or would you rather be a fish?

Photograph: Children examining their small catch at the Round Pond, Kensington, London. © Fox Photos/Hulton Archive/Getty Images

Quotation: From song Swinging on a Star 1944. Johny Burke (1908 - 1964)

One does not miss
any chance to hold onto

**the things that are
really precious,**

if one is truly wise.

Painting: The Favourite by George Stevens, (1810 - 1865) Private Collection/
Photo © Bonhams, London, UK/ The Bridgeman Art Library

Quotation: Ed Greenwood www.quotationspage.com

Six year old twins

Oliver and Anthony,
hold two sets of twin lambs
that are only a few weeks old.

Let sleeping dogs lie

Painting: A Sleeping Dog with Terracotta Pot, 1650 (oil on panel)
by Gerard Dou (1613 - 1675) The Bridgeman Art Library/Getty Images

Quotation: Traditional proverb

Winning

sn't everything...

Old age means realizing
you will never own
all the dogs you wanted to.

Drawings: Irish Wolfhound, West Highlander and Cairn, 1930,
Illustrations from his Sketch Book used for 'Just Among Friends',
Aldin, Cecil Charles Windsor (1870 - 1935), later Published by Eyre
and Spottiswoode Limited, 1934, Chalk and Charcoal on paper.
Private Collection/The Stapleton Collection/ The Bridgeman Art Library

Quotation: Joe Gores www.quotationspage.com

Irish wolfhounds
West Highlander

The kinkajou

is sometimes known as the honey bear.

Native to the rainforests of Central and South America, they are seldom seen by people because of their strict nocturnal habits.

Kinkajous are sometimes kept as pets as they are playful, generally quiet and docile.

Kinkajous dislike being awake during the day, and dislike noise and sudden movements.

National Trust Warden
Dave Morris (right) with his ferrets

and Dave's son Oliver (above)
with his pet snake Charlie.
Charlie is an Irian Jaya Carpet Python

I like pigs.
Dogs look up to us.
Cats look down on us.

Pigs treat us as equals.

Photograph: Three Royal Navy sailors from HMS Excellent holding pigs at Whale Island, Portsmouth. © Fox Photos/Hulton Archive/HGetty Image

Quotation: Sir Winston Churchill
British politician (1874 - 1965) www.quotationspage.com

Two Horses Heads, 'Mill Reef' (litho) by Skeaping, John Rattenbury (1901 - 1980)
Private Collection. © Nick Skeaping/The British Sporting Art Trust/
The Bridgeman Art Library

John Skeaping (64—150)

Photographs: Animal Photography/Sally Anne Thompson

Nine St Bernard puppies
eating from their bowls
as their mother
watches over them

Photographs: © Willie Vanderson/Hulton Archive/Getty Images

I told the folks, yet wondered why

No one could see the mouse but I

I've been sneaking out at night,

I've been sneaking out,
looking for lions.

But,
don't tell anyone.
If they knew,
they'd put a stop to it.

Last night,
I thought I heard a distant roar.
I don't know though,
it might have just been a car
off in the distance.
I'm sure I'll find a lion or two,
if I just keep looking.

I'm sneaking out again tonight,
and tomorrow night too.
I'm going to find a damn lion if it kills me.
I know they're out there,
somewhere,
I can't be the only one.

**Pictures
to share**

Acknowledgements
Our thanks to the many contributors who have allowed
their text or imagery to be used for a reduced or no fee.
Thanks also to Blue Leaf Communications whose help with
the design of the book has been invaluable.

Thanks to our sponsors

ANDREWS CHARITABLE TRUST

Published by
Pictures to Share Community Interest Company.
Peckforton, Cheshire
www.picturestoshare.co.uk

Printed in England by
Burlington Press
Station Road, Foxton, Cambridge CB22 6SA